MW01598533

# CONTENTS

### DID YOU KNOW?

*Ocean salt alone possesses the power to restore*
*wholeness to the human internal seas, our body fluids.*

# SALT ROCKS!

### Make every meal a fine dining experience

VIRGINIA MARION

◆ FriesenPress

Suite 300 - 990 Fort St
Victoria, BC, Canada, V8V 3K2
www.friesenpress.com

**Copyright © 2015 by Virginia Marion**
First Edition — 2015

All rights reserved.

No part of this publication may be reproduced in any form, or by any means, electronic
or mechanical, including photocopying, recording, or any information browsing, storage,
or retrieval system, without permission in writing from FriesenPress.

*www.thesaltcellar.ca*

**ISBN**
978-1-4602-7191-9 (Hardcover)
978-1-4602-7192-6 (Paperback)
978-1-4602-7193-3 (eBook)

*1. Cooking*

Distributed to the trade by The Ingram Book Company

# ACKNOWLEDGEMENTS

*I would like to give special thanks to the following people for their
invaluable contributions that made me realize the dream of creating my first cookbook.*

*To my partner, Will Hamm, whose faith and encouragement
has brought me to this amazing point in my life.*

*To my son, Luke Houlihan, whose practical wisdom has kept me focused.*

*To my son, Kayle Houlihan, for his words of encouragement and praise.*

*To my sister, Elizabeth Marion, for all of her sound business advice.*

*To my nephew, Billy Everitt, for his creative insight.*

*To Jacquie Dallas for faithfully using my products in all of her cooking endeavors.*

*To Alice D'Eon for having the sweetest voice in my cheering section.*

*To my long-time friend, Joan Ward, for making me feel so proud of my accomplishments.*

*To Corrie Hamm for her creativity in making my logo a work of art.*

*To Sue Herron for being a true friend, helping me in every phase of my business.*

*To Vicky May for stepping up to the plate when I needed a helping hand.*

*To Dawn Maurer for her wit and cooking suggestions.*

*To Vinnie for guiding me through the technical chaos.*

*To Natalie and Shane Viklund for providing photos of salt that look good enough to eat.
Their photography can be seen at elegantimages.ca.*

*To my mum and dad—an ever presence.*

*To all of my customers.*

## DID YOU KNOW?

*There is an enormous salt mine under the city of Detroit, about 1,000 feet below ground. According to the Detroit Salt Co., the century old mine spreads out more that 1,500 acres and has more than 100 miles of underground roads.*

# TESTIMONIALS

At Añejo Restaurant I've used a variety of salts since our inception two and a half years ago. I use four different types on our regular menu, and a great variety of others for special events. A fine finishing salt is key to a well-balanced and complete dish, and I use them on everything from fresh ceviches to savoury molé chickens. I have found no salt of better quality and variety than at The Salt Cellar.

**Matt Davidson**
*Chef de Cuisine, Añejo Restaurant*

The Smuggler's Group of restaurants has been in a partnership with The Salt Cellar for several years now. The team always comes up with new and interesting ways for us to utilize their products, whether it be a current item or a new line of salts and sugars. The Salt Cellar is widely used in our multi-unit operation and has played a major role in setting us apart.

**Gary Hennessey**
*Corporate Chef, Smuggler's Group of Restaurants*

Every year end we say thank you to our top-selling customers with a special gift. This past year we gave artisanal salts and blends created by chef and seasoning wizard Virginia Marion, owner and operator of The Salt Cellar. This seemed like the perfect gift to us because of the importance of salt in adrenal fatigue and our company's focus on this stress problem. Our customers' response was overwhelmingly enthusiastic! People were excited to find how amazing these salts and blends made everything taste.

**Dr. James Wilson**
*Future Formulations, Tucson, Arizona*

Virginia's fantastic salt blends inspire cocktail parties.
Virginia's imaginative salt blends inspire kitchen parties.
Virginia's finishing salts are a must for chefs and culinary enthusiasts.

**Raegan and Elana**
*Mountain Mercato, Canmore, Alberta*

DID YOU KNOW?

*Salt is a natural antihistamine. A pinch of salt sprinkled on the tongue may help improve an allergic reaction or an asthma attack.*

# AN INTRODUCTION
## TO THE WORLD OF GOURMET SALTS

*Whether you're trying out a few new, easy to follow recipes or using your own traditional ones, this book will change the way you think about food.*

*Once you've tried a few of these artisan salts, you will be hooked. Food has never tasted so good.*

*We are passionate about salt.*

SODIUM INTAKE HAS LONG BEEN A HEATED TOPIC in medical circles and around dinner tables. How much salt is too much? How much is not enough?

We can all agree consuming processed foods can spike our sodium intake to unhealthy levels. But by avoiding processed foods we can safely put our salt consumption back into our own hands—where it belongs.

Over time salt has been over-processed to the point it has been stripped of all its inherent goodness. It is now often thought of as solely a preservative in canned foods, meats and ready-to-eat meals.

During the refining process to produce common table salt, the trace minerals found in the sea are removed. What happens to these minerals? Well, they are often sold to companies that produce nutritional supplements.

Sea salts contain the precious minerals our bodies require to function, such as sulphur, magnesium, manganese, potassium, calcium, iron, zinc and copper.

All of the salts referred to in this book are hand-harvested in the ancient Celtic tradition and are Kosher certified. They are solar evaporated to retain their high mineral content. Because of this, salt can once again be used for what it was intended— to regulate our bodily functions and safely flavour our food.

Isn't hand-harvested sea salt a better choice?

## DID YOU KNOW?

*Unrefined sea salt is a better choice of salt because ordinary table salt is stripped of its companion elements. Aluminum silicate is added keep it powdery and porous. Aluminum is a very toxic element in our nervous system. It is implicated as one of the primary causes of Alzheimer's disease.*

# MINERAL SALTS

THERE ARE MANY SALTS FROM AROUND THE WORLD that have a high mineral content but for the purposes of this book, The Salt Cellar has chosen the most well-known and readily available. The mentioned salts are high in mineral content. Nothing has been added or taken away.

All of our salts—whether pure, infused, smoked or blended—are hand-harvested in the ancient Celtic tradition. This means wooden tools are used to gather the salt—not heavy-duty machines that may destroy its delicate balance. All salts are solar-evaporated; they are not subject to harsh processing, which strips away its nutrients leaving only sodium.

When you're looking to introduce clean, healthy salts into your diet, feel confident in choosing any or all of the following:

**Alaea**™ is a traditional Hawaiian table salt great for rubs and spice blends. Volcanic-baked red clay is a natural mineral, which is added to the salt to enrich it with iron oxide. The Hawaiians use it to seal in the moisture and add flavor. It has a mellow flavour.

**Himalayan Pink** is a mined salt from deep in the Andes. It has been proclaimed to be one of the healthiest salts in the world containing eighty-four trace minerals. Some of the minerals include zinc, calcium, magnesium, manganese, iron potassium and iodine. Pink Himalayan has many health applications but you can use this one in everyday cooking and as a table salt.

**Hiwa Kai**™ is another Hawaiian salt. It is infused with activated charcoal and is considered to have detoxifying health benefits.

**Kosher Salt** is more of a flake than a granule, and therefore dissolves more easily. Because of its flakiness, there is a lot less sodium in a spoon of Kosher salt than there is in ordinary table salt.

**Sel Gris de Guérande** is an everyday salt used to replace your ordinary table salt. This salt gets its name from its light grey colour, which is due to the clay found in the salt flats from the coastal areas of France. The coarse grey is very high in mineral content. All of its nutrients are still intact from the wealth of nutrients in the ocean.

DID YOU KNOW?

*Salt cod was the leading cargo carried from North America to the Caribbean. It was used to feed slaves on sugar plantations.*

# BLENDS

USING OUR BLENDED SALTS TAKES THE GUESSWORK out of food preparation. Our blends have been tested in many recipes and have been found to bring out the inherent flavor of the foods being cooked.

We use only the finest ingredients to make our blends. They are all preservative, additive and gluten free.

The recipes and recipe suggestions are just that—suggestions. Throw caution to the wind. Experiment with them all. You are only limited by your imagination.

DID YOU KNOW?

*"Glitter" is 1950's slang for salt.*

# ACADIAN CAJUN

A DELICIOUS BLEND OF HERBS AND SPICES
WITH JUST THE RIGHT AMOUNT OF HEAT.

## BARBECUE CHICKEN WINGS

1. Rinse **2 lbs wings** under cold water. Pat dry.
2. If wings are whole, split in half. Chop off the wing tip; save for stock.
3. Toss wings with a good sprinkle of **Acadian Cajun** in a large bowl.
4. Cook on the barbecue, turning once or twice until wings are cooked through, about 15 minutes.

**Substitute:** *Canadian Bacon, Black & White, Lime Pepper*

## YAM FRIES

1. Take **1 or 2 yams** and scrub under cold running water. Slice into fries; not too thin as they will burn.
2. Toss fries in about **1 tablespoon extra-virgin olive oil**. This will help the spice rub to stick.
3. Sprinkle on a generous amount of **Acadian Cajun** and toss to coat.
4. Bake in a 400°F oven for about 15 minutes or until the fries are starting to brown.

**Substitute:** *Chilli Sea Salt, Roasted Garlic, Black Truffle, Toasted Onion*

**Other favourites:** *Barbecued shrimp, jambalaya.*

DID YOU KNOW?

*In the early 1800s salt was 4 times as expensive as beef on the frontier. It was essential in keeping people and livestock alive.*

# BLACK & WHITE

A UNIQUE COMBINATION OF FRENCH GREY SEA SALT AND SMOKED PEPPER.
USE AS A TABLE CONDIMENT OR AS A SIMPLE RUB ON ROASTS AND STEAKS.
YOU'LL LOVE IT ON EVERYTHING.

## ORZO PILAF

1. Combine **2 cups of cooked orzo**, **¼ cup crumbled feta cheese**, **¼ cup finely chopped red onion**, **¼ cup finely chopped carrot**, **3 tablespoons chopped flat-leafed parsley**, **1 tablespoon red wine vinegar**, **1 tablespoon extra-virgin olive oil** and a **¼ teaspoon Black & White**.
2. Toss well to coat.
3. Serve immediately as a main or side dish, or cool and serve as a salad.

**Substitute:** *Oregano Blend, Lime Pepper, Black Truffle*

## ROASTED TOMATO SAUCE

1. Place approximately **2 lbs halved ripe tomatoes** on a large baking tray.
2. Slice **3 garlic cloves** and scatter around the tomatoes.
3. Add a few **thyme sprigs**. Season with **Black & White**.
4. Drizzle with **5 tablespoons of extra-virgin olive oil** and a **pinch of sugar**.
5. Roast at 350°F for 1 hour.
6. Put into a processor and blend until smooth.

**Substitute:** *Oregano Blend, Merlot-Infused Sea Salt, Toasted Onion*

**Other favourites:** *Irish stew, meat loaf, steak.*

DID YOU KNOW?

*Most people should limit their salt intake to 2,300 mg a day.*

# CANADIAN BACON?

PURE MAPLE SYRUP FROM QUEBEC MAKES THIS BLEND VERY SPECIAL.
IT TASTES LIKE BACON YET CONTAINS NO BACON—MAKING IT A HEALTHIER SALT BLEND.
YOU'RE GOING TO WANT TO PUT THIS ON EVERYTHING.

## PARSNIP CHIPS WITH MAPLE MUSTARD

1. Peel **one parsnip** per person and then cut into chunky chips. Roast with **sunflower oil** and **Canadian Bacon** at 350°F for 20-30 minutes until crispy and golden.
2. For dipping: Mix **crème fraîche** with **2 tablespoons grainy mustard**, **2 tablespoons pure maple syrup** and some extra **Canadian Bacon.**

**Substitute:** *Roasted Garlic, Habanero, Yakima*

## CRÈME FRAÎCHE

1. In a bowl, combine **2 tablespoons of buttermilk** or **yogurt** and **1 cup of heavy cream**.
2. Cover with a clean kitchen cloth in a warm, draft-free place and let sit until thickened but still a pourable consistency—about 12 to 16 hours.
3. Stir and refrigerate until ready to use (Can be refrigerated for up to 1 week.).

## CORN ON THE COB

1. Place your favorite shucked **corn on the cob** on a piece of tin foil. Pour on melted **unsalted butter** and sprinkle with **1 tablespoon Canadian Bacon**. Roll cobs to coat well.
2. Grill on the barbecue until the maple sugar in the Canadian Bacon has caramelized.

**Substitute:** *Chili Salt, Lime Pepper, Holy Smoke*

**Other favourites:** *Popcorn, roasted root vegetables, pork tenderloin, grilled salmon, scrambled eggs.*

## DID YOU KNOW?

*If you need to prepare a leafy salad in advance, lightly salt the salad immediately after you prepare it, and it will remain crisp for several hours.*

# CHILI SALT

BASED ON AN AUTHENTIC THAI RECIPE.
THIS SALTY-SWEET COMBINATION PROVIDES
THE RIGHT AMOUNT OF HEAT.

## NACHOS

1. Spread a few handfuls of **tortilla chips** on a large platter. Top with **1 cup shredded cheese**, **chopped green onions**, **sliced olives**, **sliced hot peppers**, and a sprinkle of **Chili Salt**.
2. Bake in oven at 350°F until cheese melts.

**Substitute:** *Canadian Bacon, Habanero, Sriracha*

## CHILI FRIES

1. You can use **frozen fries** here if you want a shortcut. Otherwise, get some fresh **Yukon Gold potatoes** and cut them into fries. Partially cook them in **oil** for 3-5 minutes. Drain well and place on a large baking sheet.
2. Sprinkle with **1 cup roasted chopped chillies**, **1 cup shredded jalapeño jack cheese** and **2 teaspoons Chili Salt.**
3. Bake for about 20 minutes or until fries are starting to color.

**Substitute:** *Habanero, Sriracha*

**Other favourites:** *Fresh fruit, eggs, baked beans, popcorn.*

DID YOU KNOW?

*That the majority of the sodium consumed is from processed and restaurant foods?*

# LIME PEPPER

LIME, SEA SALT AND FRESH CRACKED PEPPER CAN BE
SPRINKLED OR RUBBED ON JUST ABOUT EVERYTHING.
IT WILL BRING YOUR DISHES A CLEAN CITRUS TASTE.

## SUMMER SQUASH RIBBONS

1. Shave **3 small zucchini** and **3 small yellow squash** into ribbons using a vegetable peeler, stopping at the seeds. Place ribbons in a large bowl. In a small bowl combine **¼ teaspoon grated lime rind**, **1 tablespoon fresh lime juice**, **two minced garlic cloves** and **½ teaspoon Lime Pepper**. Combine with a whisk.
2. Add to ribbon slices and gently toss.
3. Sprinkle with **¼ cup shaved fresh parmesan cheese**.

**Substitute:** *Oh Chihuahua, Black & White*

## MINI AVOCADO TARTS

1. Buy mini **croustade cases** from your local grocery store and scoop a small **spoonful of yogurt or sour cream** into each.
2. Finely dice **2 ripe avocadoes** and mix with a little **lime juice**, some **poppy seeds** and finely snipped **chives**. Pile on top of sour cream.
3. Sprinkle each croustade with a little **Lime Pepper**.

**Substitute:** *Black Truffle, Toasted Onion, Chili Salt*

**Other favourites:** *Ahi tuna, Caesar salad, quesadillas, wings.*

DID YOU KNOW?

*Your body needs 200mg a day to be healthy.*

# OH CHIHUAHUA

MESQUITE FROM THE CHIHUAHUA REGION OF MEXICO IS USED TO MAKE THIS EXQUISITE BLEND. IT HAS BEEN TEMPERED WITH FRESH LIME AND ORGANIC OREGANO.

## CUCUMBER SALMON

1. Cut **1 large cucumber** into 20 thick slices and scoop out some of the seedy middle, leaving a dip.
2. Mix **¾ cup Crème Fraîche** (recipe under Canadian Bacon) with the **zest of 1 lemon** and **½ teaspoon Oh Chihuahua.**
3. Spoon the mixture into the dip of the cucumber slices. Top with **smoked salmon**.

**Substitutes:** *Lime Pepper, Black & White, Curried Sea Salt*

## ASPARAGUS HAM ROLLS

1. Preheat oven to 400°F. Peel the lower third, and remove tough ends, of **1 lb of white asparagus** and **1 lb of green asparagus**. Cook in **boiling water** for about 8 minutes.
2. Remove asparagus from water and drain well.
3. Mixing the colours, place 3 or 4 asparagus spears on a slice of **Serrano ham**. (You will need about **¾ lb of the ham** altogether). Roll up the ham and spears. Place the rolls next to each other in a casserole dish.
4. Slice a few **tomatoes**. Place the slices on top of the ham rolls. Sprinkle with **Oh Chihuahua** and **¾ lb grated Gouda**. Bake for 15 minutes. Sprinkle with **chopped parsley**.

**Substitutes:** *Lime Pepper, Canadian Bacon, Salish Alderwood Smoked*

**Other favourites:** *Grilled Portobello, ribs, black bean burgers, tomato soup.*

DID YOU KNOW?

*Adequate salt consumption encourages a
healthy weight and a fast metabolism.*

# OREGANO BLEND

A DELICIOUS ORGANIC COMBINATION OF SALT AND SPICES.
EXCELLENT WITH ITALIAN AND GREEK CUISINE.

## PIZZA ARRABIATA

1. Prepare your favorite **dough** recipe.
2. Heat a large skillet over medium heat. Add **2 ounces of chopped pancetta**. Cook for 5 minutes. Remove from pan and discard drippings.
3. Add **1 tablespoon extra-virgin olive oil**. Add **2/3 cup chopped onion, ½ teaspoon crushed red pepper, 4 thinly-sliced garlic cloves**. Cook until onion is translucent. Add **2 medium diced tomatoes** and a sprinkle of **Oregano Blend**. Simmer one minute.
4. Spread the fresh-made sauce on the pizza dough. Sprinkle with **¾ cup shredded mozzarella cheese** and the pancetta.
5. Bake at 500°F for 10 minutes or until the crust is browned.

**Substitute:** *Canadian Bacon*

## LEMON OREGANO LAMB CHOPS

1. Combine **2 tablespoons of fresh lemon juice, 1 teaspoon extra-virgin olive oil, ½ teaspoon Oregano Blend** and **2 cloves of minced garlic** in a Ziploc bag.
2. Add **4 lamb chops** to bag, turning to coat. Seal and marinate for 15 minutes at room temperature.
3. Remove lamb and cook the chops your favourite way, 3 minutes on each side.

**Substitute:** *Rosemary Sea Salt*

**Other favourites:** *Greek salad, linguini with extra-virgin olive oil and parmesan cheese, omelettes.*

### DID YOU KNOW?

*By listening to your body's salt cravings, it will tell you how much salt to consume.*

# SMOKN' GUNS

HABANERO, LIME AND SMOKE.
USE IT ON ANYTHING YOU WANT TO KICK UP.

## DEVILED EGGS

1. Boil **1 dozen eggs** for 10 minutes. Peel off shell, cut in half and scoop the yolk into a bowl.
2. Mash yolks with enough **mayonnaise** to get a good consistency. Add a splash of **Worcestershire sauce**, **1 teaspoon dry mustard** and **½ teaspoon Smokn' Guns**. Mix well.
3. Spoon the mixture into egg whites or use a piping bag. Sprinkle with **freshly chopped dill**.

**Substitute:** *Black & White, Lime Sea Salt, Curried Sea Salt*

## SPICY PRAWN SKEWERS

1. Marinate **½ lb cooked prawns** in the **zest and juice of 1 lime**, **1 tablespoon soya sauce**, **½ a finely chopped chili** and **1 teaspoon clear honey** for 20 minutes.
2. To serve, lay each prawn on a **baby spinach leaf** and thread through a cocktail skewer.
3. Sprinkle with **Smokn' Guns**.

**Substitute:** *Ginger Sea Salt, Sriracha*

**Other favourites:** *Yam fries, scrambled eggs.*

DID YOU KNOW?

*There are over 14,000 different uses for salt, from removing stains to easing sprains.*

# LEMON DILL

FRESH LEMON JUICE AND NATURAL SEA SALT MAKE UP THIS A WINNING COMBINATION.
ADD IT TO FRESH SALADS, FISH AND SEAFOOD—OR ON ANYTHING WHERE YOU WANT A PURE CITRUS TASTE.

## MUSHROOM HERB SALAD

1. Sauté **3 minced strips of thick-sliced bacon** in a skillet over medium heat until crisp; drain on a paper towel-lined plate.
2. Whisk **¼ cup fresh lemon juice**, **2 teaspoon extra-virgin olive oil**, **¼ teaspoon Lemon Dill**, and **fresh ground pepper** together in a large bowl.
3. Add reserved bacon, **½ lb of thinly sliced Cremini mushrooms**, **½ cup fresh parsley leaves** and **½ cup fresh mint leaves**. Toss to coat.

**Substitute:** *Lime Pepper Salt, Lime Sea Salt*

## CITRUS MOZZARELLA BITES

1. In a bowl, mix **1 container of drained bocconcini**, the **zest of 1 lemon**, **3 tablespoons extra-virgin olive oil**, **2 table-spoons finely chopped fresh basil**, **Lemon Dill**, and **fresh-ground black pepper** to taste.
2. Chill for approximately one hour.

**Substitute:** *Lime Sea Salt, Lime Pepper, Habanero*

**Other favourites:** *Caesar salad, omelettes, fresh salads dressed with oil & vinegar.*

Habanero

110g

Roasted Garlic

110g

ack Truffle

100 g

Lime Fresco Sea S

100 g

DID YOU KNOW?

*"He is not worth his salt" is a common expression. It originated in ancient Greece where salt was traded for slaves.*

# INFUSED SEA SALTS

THE FLAVOURED SALTS USED AT THE SALT CELLAR have been infused with one other natural ingredient, such as roasted garlic, habanero peppers or fresh lime. That's it! Two ingredients. No additives or preservatives. It doesn't get much purer than that.

So how do you spell delicious?

Drizzle your fish with a little extra-virgin olive oil and then experiment with a sprinkle of Lime Sea Salt or Ginger Sea Salt.

Put a dash of Merlot-Infused Sea Salt in your cheese fondue.

Sprinkled Toasted Onion on a crisp oil and vinegar salad. It's amazing!

Black Truffle anyone? Try it on almost anything! But it's especially good on creamy pastas—or our personal favourite: Popcorn!

Most of the infused salts in this book are best used as a finishing salt. This means using the salt at the end of cooking when the dish is ready to be served. There are a few exceptions when you can add them just before you finish cooking to get the benefit of the salt's full flavour.

Remember: A little goes a long way.

DID YOU KNOW?

*Salt improves sleep quality.*

# BLACK TRUFFLE

IMPORTED FROM ITALY, THIS STRONG FLAVORED SEA SALT IS A REAL TREAT.

## ROASTED SALMON FILLETS

1. Preheat oven to 450°F. Place **4 salmon fillets** on a heavy-duty baking sheet. Brush with **extra-virgin olive oil** and sprinkle with **Black Truffle**.
2. Roast fish for 8-10 minutes. Turn off heat and let stand in unopened oven for 3-5 minutes longer.

**Substitutes:** *Canadian Bacon, Acadian Cajun, Oregano Blend*

## BACON MASHED POTATOES

1. Mash **2 lbs of Yukon Gold potatoes** with **3 tablespoons unsalted butter** and a **¼ cup light cream** until creamy smooth.
2. Sprinkle in **½ teaspoon Black Truffle Sea Salt** and **¼ cup chopped green onions**.
3. Add **3 slices of well-cooked bacon**, crumbled (Turkey bacon can be used as a substitute.).

**Substitutes:** *Canadian Bacon, Roasted Garlic*

**Other favourites:** *Eggs, pasta, stuffed mushrooms, popcorn.*

DID YOU KNOW?

*A typical serving of whole wheat bread has 132g mg of sodium. The average oat-bran bagel contains 532 mg of sodium.*

# CHIPOTLE

MADE WITH REAL SMOKE-DRIED JALAPEÑO PEPPERS.

## CHEESEBURGERS

1. Prepare and heat the grill.
2. In a medium bowl, combine **1 lb of ground beef or ground lamb** with **½ teaspoon of Chipotle Sea Salt** and mix gently. Shape into 4 patties.
3. Grill for about 7 minutes on one side. Flip, cook other side for 3-4 minutes more.
4. Top with **1½ cups of grated Colby or cheddar cheese**. Cook until cheese is melted.
5. Top with your favorite ingredients.

**Substitute:** *Sriracha, Habanero*

## TOMATO SANDWICH WITH BLACKBERRY CHIPOTLE MAYONNAISE

1. In a blender, puree **1 cup of fresh blackberries** with **½ teaspoon of Chipotle Sea Salt**. Combine with **1 cup of mayonnaise**.
2. Fry **16 bacon strips** until crisp. Drain, leaving about **1 tablespoon bacon grease** in the pan.
3. Thinly slice **1 medium red onion** and cook over low heat until golden brown.
4. Spread the blackberry chipotle sauce on one side of each piece of bread and assemble sandwich with bacon, onions, **tomato** and **lettuce**.

**Substitute:** *Lemon Dill, Habanero, Sriracha*

**Other favourites:** *Grilled vegetables, seafood salad, frittatas.*

## DID YOU KNOW?

*The Naga Jolokia pepper is named for one of the most venomous snakes in India, and is also known as the King Cobra Chili.*

SALT
cellar

Ghost Pepper
Naga Jolokia a infusé du sel marin
Sprinkle over chicken wings, chili or fajita.

Caution: Extremely Hot
Hand-harvested, unrefined sea salts.
No additives or preservatives. Gluten-free.
Store in a cool, dry place.
For recipe ideas & nutritional info please visit: www.thesaltcellar.ca

# GHOST PEPPER

WE DARE YOU!
MADE FROM ONE OF THE HOTTEST PEPPERS IN THE WORLD, THE NAGA JOLOKIA,
THIS SALT'S HEAT WILL MAKE YOUR TOES CURL.

## SPICY MASHED SWEET POTATOES

1. Boil **2 lbs of peeled and cubed sweet potatoes** in a large saucepan of **salted water** until tender—about 15 minutes. Drain, return potatoes to pan, and dry briefly over medium heat, stirring constantly.
2. Mash **3 tablespoons unsalted butter** and **1 teaspoon brown sugar** into potatoes using a potato masher. Season with the **Ghost Pepper Salt** and **freshly ground pepper**.
3. Sprinkle with **fresh jalapeños**, if desired.

**Substitute:** *Habanero, Sriracha, Smokn' Guns*

## SPICY SHRIMP

1. Use paper towels to pat dry **12 large peeled and deveined shrimp**, leaving on the tails, then toss with **1 tablespoon olive oil**.
2. Combine **1½ teaspoon paprika, ½ teaspoon ground turmeric** and a **¼ teaspoon Ghost Pepper Salt** in a small bowl. Sprinkle over shrimp.
3. Coat a grill pan or large sauté pan with a non-stick spray and heat over medium-high. Cook until the shrimp turn pink and are cooked through, 1-2 minutes per side.

**Substitute:** *Habanero, Sriracha*

**Other favourites:** *Chili, fajitas.*

DID YOU KNOW?

*The only true necessity, physiologically speaking is salt. The sodium it provides regulates the heartbeat and the body's balance of fluids.*

# HABANERO

TURN UP THE HEAT WITH HIGH QUALITY HABANEROS, JUST SO YOU CAN LOVE YOUR FOOD A LITTLE MORE. USE ON ANYTHING WHERE YOU WANT THAT EXTRA KICK.

## BACON-WRAPPED JALAPEÑO POPPERS

1. Sprinkle about **½ teaspoon of Habanero Salt** into **14-16 oz of cream cheese**.
2. Fill **25 halved and seeded fresh jalapeños** with the cream cheese mixture.
3. Wrap each jalapeño with a half-strip of **bacon** (a package of bacon should do it.).
4. Lay out in a dish large enough to hold all of the jalapeños.
5. Sprinkle **2 cups grated cheddar cheese** on top.
6. Cook in a preheated oven of 450°F for 10-15 minutes, until bacon is fully cooked.

**Substitute***: Ghost Pepper, Sriracha*

## SALSA VERDE

1. Roast **3 long chillies** over an open flame or in the oven at 400°F.
2. Steam the chillies in a paper bag or in a bowl covered with a plate.
3. Rub away the burned peel. Stem and seed the chillies and coarsely chop them. There should be about ½ cup.
4. In a medium saucepan, cover **1 lb (about 12) husked tomatillos** with **water**. Set the pan over medium heat, bring to a simmer. Cook uncovered for about 10 minutes or until the tomatillos are soft. Drain and let them cool.
5. In a blender, combine the tomatillos, green chillies, water, **2 cloves garlic**, and **Habanero Salt.** Purée on high-speed until smooth.
6. Transfer to a bowl and stir in **½ cup chopped white onion** and **¼ cup minced fresh cilantro or basil**. Cover and refrigerate.

**Substitute:** *Smokn' Guns, Sriracha*

**Other favourites:** *Chowders, spicy shrimp, mac & cheese.*

*That some sea salt contains additives? Kosher salt typically does not have any additives or anti-caking agents.*

# LIME SEA SALT

THE NATURAL FLAVOR OF LIME IS AN INTERNATIONAL FAVORITE.
THAI FOOD, MARGARITAS, DESSERTS—THE USES ARE PLENTIFUL.
REFRESHING AND VERSATILE, LIME SEA SALT IS TART WITHOUT BEING TOO SOUR.

## MARGARITA CROSTINI

1. Preheat broiler to high with rack 3-4" from the element. Coat a baking sheet with non-stick spray. Arrange **eight ½"-thick rounds from a baguette** on the baking sheet.
2. Top **the** baguette rounds with **¼"-thick tomatoes slices**. Season with **Lime Sea Salt**, and then top each round with **a slice of fresh mozzarella cheese**.
3. Broil until cheese melts and begins to bubble—3-5 minutes. Watch closely to prevent burning.
4. Remove from oven and top each crostini with **leaves fresh basil** before serving.

**Substitute:** *Lime Pepper, Lemon Sea Salt, Habanero*

## MANGO SALSA

1. Peel, pit and dice **1 ripe mango**.
2. Finely chop **½ medium red onion**, **1 jalapeño** (seeds and ribs removed), **1 small cucumber**, **1 small red pepper** and **3 tablespoons chopped fresh cilantro**.
3. Put all ingredients into a small bowl and squeeze in **3 tablespoons fresh lime juice**.
4. Sprinkle with **½ teaspoon Lime Sea Salt.** Blend well.
5. Serve with fish or chicken.

**Substitute:** *Lime Pepper, Sriracha*

**Other favourites:** *Guacamole, tzatziki, fish (grilled, broiled or pan-fried).*

DID YOU KNOW?

*In Gujarati culture, salt is supposed to be the first purchase made for a wedding.*

# ROASTED GARLIC

INFUSED WITH REAL GARLIC. NEED WE SAY MORE?
SPRINKLE IT ON ALMOST ANYTHING.

## PITA CHIPS

1. Preheat broiler to high.
2. Combine **1 teaspoon Roasted Garlic**, **½ teaspoon paprika**, and **cayenne** to taste in a small bowl. Set aside.
3. Lightly brush **4 split rounds of pita bread** with **olive oil** on one side and sprinkle with seasoning mixture.
4. Cut pitas in half, then in half again and then in half again until you have 8 chips per pita.
5. Transfer pitas to a baking sheet and broil until golden, about 2 minutes.

**Substitute:** *Toasted Onion, Canadian Bacon*

## BABY POTATOES WITH GREEK YOGURT AND CHOPPED CHIVES

1. Bake **24 potatoes** until tender, about 20-30 minutes, depending on size.
2. Using a small knife, make a cross in the top of each one and then use your thumbs and forefinger to squeeze it gently open. Sprinkle a **pinch of Roasted Garlic** into each potato.
3. Mix together **2 tablespoons of chives** and about **3½ ounces plain Greek yogurt**. Top each potato with the yogurt mix.
4. Sprinkle with **black or red caviar** for a special occasion.

**Substitute:** *Oh Chihuahua, Rosemary Sea Salt, Canadian Bacon*

**Other favourites:** *Hummus, mashed potatoes, roasted chicken.*

**DID YOU KNOW?**

*Cream will whip better if you add a pinch of salt.*

# ROSEMARY SEA SALT

SO FRESH IT TASTES LIKE YOU JUST PICKED IT.

## VEGGIE BURGERS

These delicious hot sandwiches have a very meaty taste, even though there's no meat in them!

1. In a food processor, pulse or blend until coarsely chopped, a **15 ounce can of rinsed and drained black beans**, **¾ cup rolled oats**, **½ cup fresh mushrooms**, **1 chopped onion**, **1 shredded carrot**, **½ cup chopped red bell pepper**, and **3 garlic cloves**. Do NOT purée.
2. Blend in **5 tablespoons chili sauce**, **½ teaspoon Rosemary Sea Salt** and **1/8 teaspoon white pepper**.
3. Chill mixture, then shape into four 1/2"-thick patties. Cook immediately, or wrap and freeze.
4. Cook your favorite way, either in the oven, on the barbecue or on top of the stove.

**Substitute:** *Canadian Bacon*, *Oh Chihuahua*

## TOMATO-ROSEMARY FLATBREAD

1. Brush a fresh piece of **flatbread** with **2 tablespoons extra-virgin olive oil** mixed with **½ teaspoon finely chopped rosemary**. Prick the flatbread all over with a fork.
2. In a small bowl, mix **2/3 cup ricotta cheese**, **½ teaspoon olive oil** and a sprinkling of **fresh-ground black pepper**.
3. Spread a thin layer of the ricotta mixture over the flatbread.
4. Thinly slice **2 tomatoes** and evenly place the slices on the flatbread. Sprinkle with **Rosemary Sea Salt**.
5. Bake in a 450°F oven for 10-12 minutes. Remove from pan, cut into squares.

**Substitute:** *Lime Pepper, Oh Chihuahua, Roasted Garlic*

**Other favourites:** *Roasted chicken, roasted lamb, roasted potatoes, leek and potato soup.*

*A product is labeled sodium-free or salt-free if it has less than 5mg of sodium, according to federal guidelines.*

# CURRIED SEA SALT

AN INTRIGUING BLEND OF SPICES ARE USED TO CREATE THIS TASTY SALT. NOT TOO SPICY.

## POTATO MASALA CURRY

1. Cook **3 or 4 medium potatoes** in just enough **water** to cover, along with **½ cup of finely chopped onion** and **2 chopped green chillies,** for about 8 minutes, or until half-cooked.
2. Meanwhile, blend **2 teaspoons garam masala**, **2 tablespoons grated unsweetened coconut** and **½ ounce fresh grated ginger** in a blender. Add to the potatoes and continue to cook for about 8 more minutes until tender but not soft.
3. Heat **2 tablespoons extra-virgin olive oil** in a frying pan and add **1 teaspoon mustard seeds**. Let them sizzle for a few seconds until they have all popped. Then add another **½ cup finely chopped onion** and fry until golden. Stir into the potato curry.
4. Add **Curried Sea Salt** to taste. Sprinkle on **chopped cilantro leaves** prior to serving.

## NAAN BREAD

1. Purchase a package of good quality plain **naan bread.**
2. Mix **3 tablespoons extra-virgin olive oil** with **½ teaspoon Curried Sea Salt**.
3. Brush the mixture evenly on the pieces of naan.
4. Bake in a 350°F oven for a few minutes, until the naan is warm and soft.
5. Serve immediately.

**Substitute:** *Roasted Garlic, Smokn' Guns*

**Other favourites:** *Any curried dish, scalloped potatoes.*

DID YOU KNOW?

*Salting fish made long-range
explorations possible in the
age of sailing ships.*

- - - - - - - - - - - - - -

# SRIRACHA

A SPICY BLEND OF SUN-RIPENED CHILLIES AND SEA SALT.

## SPICED LENTIL TOMATO SOUP

1. Place **1 cup split yellow lentils** (rinsed and drained), **1 tablespoon extra-virgin olive oil**, **1 teaspoon turmeric**, **2 crushed cloves of garlic** and **10 cups of water** in a large saucepan. Bring to a boil over high heat then reduce to low and simmer with lid on for 30 minutes or until lentils are very soft. Add more water, if necessary to keep soup consistency.
2. Add **3 large chopped tomatoes** and simmer for another 30 minutes. Season to taste with **Sriracha Salt.** Stir in **¼ cup chopped cilantro** and the **juice of ½ lemon**.

**Substitute:** *Smokn' Guns, Oh Chihuahua, Chipotle*

## BROWN RICE AND AVOCADO SALAD

1. Cook **1 cup brown rice** in plenty of **boiling water** for 30 minutes until al dente (a slight bite to the rice). Drain well and set aside to cool.
2. Combine cold rice, **1 diced avocado**, **3 diced cocktail tomatoes**, **the juice of 2 limes** and **½ cup fresh chopped basil** or **oregano**.
3. Salt to taste with **Sriracha Salt** and **fresh-ground black pepper**.

**Substitute:** *Lime Pepper, Habanero, Ghost Pepper*

**Other favourites:** *Pizza, poutine, corn on the cob.*

DID YOU KNOW?

*In most Indian religions and
cultures, a gift of salt is considered
a potent symbol of good luck.*

# GINGER SEA SALT

FRESH GINGER FROM THAILAND MAKES THIS SALT A MUST-HAVE STAPLE IN YOUR CUPBOARD.

## GINGER AND WHITE BEAN VINAIGRETTE

1. Combine **3 medium minced garlic cloves, 1 tablespoon fresh ginger, ½ cup drained pickled ginger, 3 tablespoons apple cider vinegar, ¾ teaspoon Ginger Sea Salt, 3 tablespoons cane sugar** and **¼ cup cooked white beans** in a food processor or blender until finely chopped. With the motor running, add **¾ cup extra-virgin olive oil** in a slow steady stream until well-blended.
2. Cover and refrigerate. Bring to room temperature before serving.
3. Excellent on any firm fish.

**Substitute:** *Pink Himalayan, Sel Gris*

## THAI SALAD

1. Combine **3 finely chopped Roma tomatoes** with **3 tablespoons chopped cilantro, 1 finely chopped chili, 3 tablespoons fresh lime juice, 1 teaspoon light brown sugar** and **¼ teaspoon Ginger Sea Salt** in a bowl.
2. Enjoy with fish or a vegetarian burger.

**Substitute:** *Chili Salt*

**Other favourites:** *Fresh oysters, scallops, Asian stir-fry.*

DID YOU KNOW?

*Bolivia has the world's largest salt desert. The Salar de Uyuni, covers 4,085 square miles at an altitude of 12,500 ft.*

# TOASTED ONION

A RICH FLAVOR OF TOASTED ONION AND SEA SALT.

## BUTTERNUT SQUASH WITH TOASTED ONION SALT

1. Peel and seed **1 medium-sized butternut squash**. Slice into rings.
2. Spray a cookie sheet with **oil**.
3. Lay rings on sheet and brush top sides with melted **unsalted butter**.
4. Sprinkle with **Toasted Onion Salt**.
5. Bake at 400°F for 10-12 minutes or tender when poked with a fork.

**Substitute:** *Roasted Garlic, Oh Chihuahua*

## LINGUINI WITH ONION, BACON AND PARMESAN

1. In a large frying pan, cook **½ lb chopped bacon** until crisp. Remove and drain on paper towels. Pour off all but **2 tablespoons of the bacon fat**.
2. Add **1 thinly sliced onion**, ½ teaspoon dried thyme, 1/8 teaspoon dried red pepper flakes and ¼ teaspoon **Toasted Onion Sea Salt**. Cook, stirring occasionally, until onions are brown, about 10 minutes.
3. Cook **¾ lb linguini** in **salted water** for about 12 minutes. Reserve **1 cup pasta water**.
4. Drain linguini and toss with bacon and onion mixture, ¾ cup reserved pasta water, **½ cup of freshly grated Parmesan cheese**, a **¼ cup chopped parsley** and more Toasted Onion Sea Salt and **pepper**.
5. Add additional pasta water if too thick. Serve with additional parmesan.

**Substitute:** *Canadian Bacon, Lime Pepper*

**Other favourites:** *Beef pot pie, meat loaf, vegetarian loaf, grilled mushrooms.*

## DID YOU KNOW?

*When most salts are harvested, they are put through a series of harsh steps that cracks the molecular structure, robs its essential minerals and adulterates the salt with chemical additives to make it free-flowing.*

# MERLOT-INFUSED SEA SALT

INFUSED WITH MERLOT WINE, THIS SEA SALT IS NOT ONLY RICH IN COLOUR
BUT IT ADDS A SUBTLE WINE FLAVOUR TO MANY DISHES.

## FUSILLI WITH ARTICHOKE HEARTS AND PARMESAN CREAM

1. In a medium saucepan, melt **2 tablespoons unsalted butter**. Add **2 cloves minced garlic** and cook for 30 seconds. Stir in **1 cup heavy cream (35%)**, **2½ cups drained artichoke hearts**, **3/4 teaspoon Merlot-Infused Sea Salt** and **1 teaspoon ground white pepper**.
2. Cook until just heated through, about 3 minutes.
3. Cook **¾ lb of fusilli** according to package directions. Drain and toss with the cream sauce, **½ cup freshly grated parmesan cheese** and **2 tablespoons chopped chives**.

**Substitute:** *Oh Chihuahua, Oregano Blend*

## FENNEL, PEAR AND PARMESAN SALAD

1. Arrange **1 large thinly-sliced fennel bulb, 1 firm unpeeled and sliced Bosc pear** on a decorative plate.
2. Add **4 teaspoons lemon juice** and **4 teaspoons extra-virgin olive oil**. Toss to coat. Sprinkle with **Merlot-Infused Sea Salt** and **freshly-ground black pepper**.
3. Scatter **¼ cup of shaved parmesan** over the salad.

**Substitute:** *Cyprus Flake, Fleur-de-sel*

**Other favourites:** *Steak, boeuf bourguignonne*

*Salt is bleached and iodized. This refining process
makes the salt poisonous to your body because it takes
out the essential nutrients present in sun-cured salt.*

# SMOKED SALTS

NOT ALL SMOKED SALTS ARE CREATED EQUAL. Some are milder than others depending on the type of wood used. All of the smoked salts carried by The Salt Cellar are cold-smoked over untreated woods. No liquid smoke is used.

Don't be afraid to experiment on dishes that might seem a little unconventional for a smoked salt. Below are some suggestions.

**Durango® Hickory Smoked**
Smoked over premium Hickory hardwood.
Use as a dry rub on ribs, burgers, red meat, turkey.

**Fumée-de-Sel™**
Fleur-de-Sel that has been smoked over Chardonnay Oak chips.
Delicious on fruit and chicken, and in soups and sauces.

**Holy Smoke**
Naturally smoked for 14 days over 7 different kinds of wood.
Sprinkle on roasted veggies, turkey sandwiches or creamy pasta.

**Salish® Alderwood Smoked**
Naturally smoked for 48 hours.
Add a hint to a Caprese salad or use it to rim a cocktail. It's the newest rage!

**Yakima® Applewood Smoked**
Smoked over aged Applewood for a sweet taste.
Great on fish, shellfish, poultry, pork, ham, turkey, sausage—or even ice cream.

DID YOU KNOW?

*Celtic sea salt is the lowest in sodium of all the salts available and the richest in precious beneficial elements available in any salt.*

# FLAKE SALTS AND FINISHING SALTS

**Cyprus White & Cyprus Black Lava**™ are harvested from the Cyprus Sea. This salt has pyramid shaped crystals. Cyprus Black Lava™ has been infused with activated charcoal, which acts as a cleanser and aids in digestion. It's a delectable replacement for soya sauce when dining on sushi.

**Fleur-de-Sel** is collected from the top layer of the salt ponds in the Guérande region in the south of France. Fleur-de-Sel is considered to be the crème de la crème when used to finish a dish of grilled meats, fresh vegetables and salads.

**Maldon Flake** is a salt harvested in the United Kingdom. It has a pyramid-shaped crystal with a soft crunch. These delicate crystals are ideal for finishing a salad or for use as a topping on a cream soup.

**Mayan Sun**™ is harvested from one of the last mangrove sanctuaries in El Salvador. This salt is created by trapping ocean water in manmade ponds made from mineral-rich volcanic soils. This special salt is completely unrefined with no additives.

**Murray River** is a peach flake salt from the basin of the Murray River in Australia. This flaky sea salt is ideal for sprinkling on a composed salad, a chilled cucumber soup or a Vichissoise.

## DID YOU KNOW?

*True sea salt should be moist to the touch with its prism-like "mother liquor" or bitterns surrounding it.*

# COCKTAIL SALTS

AS WITH ALL OF OUR BLENDS, our premium cocktail salts are 100% natural.

### Above the Rim

Above the Rim is a premium cocktail blend that can rim the glass of any kind of margarita, Caesar, michelada or other intriguing cocktails. We promise you will have licked off the salt before you finish your drink.

### Lime, Habanero & Celery Seed

Our Lime, Habanero & Celery Seed blend was made specifically for Caesars using traditional ingredients—but without the additives and preservatives. Rest assured you will love this spicy glass rimmer.

### Lime Margarita

Our Lime Margarita blend is head and shoulders above anything you have ever tried before. We use only the highest quality lime crystals and hand-harvested sea salt. Margaritas have never tasted so good.

### Mayan Sun

One of the finest tequila bars in Calgary, Alberta, uses this salt to rim their margaritas. It has a soft texture, much like Fleur-de-sel, which grips the rim of the glass to make for a delightful sipping experience.

## DID YOU KNOW?

*There is a very common misconception that Roman soldiers were paid in salt, but in fact they were paid in normal currency.*

# INDEX

## SOUPS AND SALADS

Brown Rice and Avocado Salad (Sriracha)

Citrus Mozzarella Bites (Lemon Dill)

Fennel, Pear and Parmesan Salad (Merlot-Infused Sea Salt)

Mushroom Herb Salad (Lemon Dill)

Spiced Lentil Tomato Soup (Sriracha)

Thai Salad (Ginger Sea Salt)

## BURGERS, PIZZA AND SANDWICHES

Cheeseburgers (Chipotle)

Pizza Arrabiata (Oregano Blend)

Tomato Rosemary Flatbread (Rosemary Sea Salt)

Tomato Sandwich with Blackberry Chipotle Mayonnaise (Chipotle)

Veggie Burgers (Rosemary Sea Salt)

## ENTRÉES

Barbecue Chicken Wings (Acadian Cajun)

Fusilli with Artichoke Hearts and Parmesan Cream (Merlot-Infused Sea Salt)

Lemon Oregano Lamb Chops (Oregano Blend)

Linguini with Onion, Bacon and Parmesan (Toasted Onion)

Orzo Pilaf (Black & White)

Potato Masala Curry (Curried Sea Salt)

Roasted Salmon Filets (Black Truffle)

Spicy Prawn Skewers (Smokn' Guns)

Spicy Shrimp (Ghost Pepper)

Summer Squash Ribbons (Lime Pepper)

## SIDE DISHES

Asparagus Ham Rolls (Oh Chihuahua)

Baby Potatoes with Greek Yogurt and Chopped Chives (Roasted Garlic)

Bacon Mashed Potatoes (Black Truffle)

Butternut Squash with Toasted Onion Salt (Toasted Onion)

Chili Fries (Chili Salt)

Corn on the Cob (Canadian Bacon?)

Mango Salsa (Lime Sea Salt)

Naan Bread (Curried Sea Salt)

Orzo Pilaf (Black & White)

Parsnip Chips with Maple Mustard (Canadian Bacon)

Spicy Mashed Sweet Potatoes (Ghost Pepper)

Summer Squash Ribbons (Lime Pepper)

Yam Fries (Acadian Cajun)

## FLAKE SALTS AND MINERAL SALTS

## SMOKED SALTS

## COCKTAIL SALTS

## ACKNOWLEDGEMENTS

IMAGES BY ELEGANT IMAGES

DID YOU KNOW INFORMATION FROM
LISTVERSE.COM & FOODREPUBLIC.COM

™ SALTS ARE TRADEMARKS OF SALTWORKS, INC.

DID YOU KNOW?

*The first written reference to salt is found in
the Book of Job, recorded about 2,250 BC.*

CPSIA information can be obtained
at www.ICGtesting.com
Printed in the USA
LVOW05s2113090616

491973LV00013B/34/P

*Confirmation Preparation for Young Children*

MW01599454

# Come, Spirit of God!

## Family Book

Margaret Bick

Catherine Ecker

NOVALIS

LTP
LITURGY
TRAINING
PUBLICATIONS

# NOVALIS

© 2006 Novalis, Saint Paul University, Ottawa, Canada

**Cover:** Anna Payne-Krzyzanowski
**Design, illustration & layout:** Anna Payne-Krzyzanowski
**Editor:** Patrick Gallagher
**Photo credits:** Bill Wittman, p. 13; Bill Wittman,
p. 20 top; Corbis SC-015-0183RM, p. 20 bottom

Business Office:
Novalis
10 Lower Spadina Avenue, Suite 400
Toronto, ON M5V 2Z2

Phone: 1-800-387-7164 or 416-363-3303 ext. 239
Fax: 1-800-204-4140 or 416-363-9409
E-mail: resources@novalis.ca
www.novalis.ca

*All rights reserved. No part of this publication may be repro-
duced, stored in a retrieval system, or transmitted in any form, or
by any means, electronic, mechanical, photocopying, recording,
or otherwise, without the written permission of the publisher.*

*We acknowledge the financial support of the Government of Canada
through the Book Publishing Industry Development Program (BPIDP)
for our publishing activities.*

ISBN:2-89507-607-3 (Novalis)
Printed in Canada.

*Nihil Obstat*
Reverend Louis J. Cameli, S.T.D.
Censor Deputatus
January 4, 2006

*Imprimatur*
Bishop-elect George J. Rassas
Vicar General
Archdiocese of Chicago
January 11, 2006

*The Nihil Obstat and Imprimatur are official declarations that a book is free of doctrinal
and moral error. No implication is contained therein that those who have granted the Nihil
Obstat and Imprimatur agree with the content, opinions, or statements expressed. Nor do
they assume any legal responsibility associated with publication.*

Published in the United States of America by Liturgy Training Publications,
1800 North Hermitage Avenue,
Chicago IL 60622-1101;
1-800-933-1800,
fax 1-800-933-7094,
email orders@ltp.org.
See our website at www.ltp.org.

Come, Spirit of God!: Confirmation Preparation for Young People, Family Book
ISBN 10: 1-56854-601-7  (Liturgy Training Publications)
ISBN 13: 978-1-56854-601-8  (Liturgy Training Publications)
CSGCPF

## Acknowledgments

We would very much like to thank the following reviewers for their valuable contribution to the development of this program:

Char Deslippe, Religious Education Coordinator, Diocese of Victoria, BC • Sr.Mary-Ann Bates, Diocesan Director of Catechetics, Diocese of Prince George, BC •

Sr.Gertrude Mulholland, Our Lady of Perpetual Help Parish, Sherwood Park, AB • Susan Suttie, Religious Education Consultant, Diocese of Calgary, AB •

Sr. Lorraine Couture, Catechetics Coordinator, Rural Catechetics Office, Prince Albert, SK • Agnes Rolheiser, Rural Catechetics, Diocese of Saskatoon, Saskatoon, SK •

Carol Anne Seed, Director of Catechetics and Faith Formation, Archdiocese of Winnipeg, Winnipeg, MB • Fr. Murray Kroetsch, Saint Pius X Church, Brantford, ON •

Emily Di Fruscia, Assistant Director, Archdiocesan Office for Faith Formation, Montreal, QC • Paul Toner, Director of Liturgy, Archdiocese of Moncton, Dieppe, NB •

Madelyn Ramier, Diocesan Director of Catechetics, Diocese of Saint John, Fredericton, NB • Marilyn Sweet, Director of Programs, Archdiocese of Halifax, Halifax, NS •

Margaret Craddock, Archdiocesan Director of Catechesis, Archdiocese of St. John's, St. John's, NL •

5 4 3 2 1   10  09 08 07 06

# Table of Contents

Dear family,

It is a privilege to be allowed into your family's life as you prepare for the completion of Christian initiation.

In confirmation, God continues and deepens the transformation begun in baptism and prepares us for life at the table of the eucharist and in the world. The rituals we will celebrate together will echo the baptism celebration and help your child reflect on that important event. The journey we take together will help your family "remember" baptism in a new way and help your child answer God's call to live as a confirmed Christian.

We offer this book to accompany you and your child on this journey. In it you will find suggestions for activities and prayers to share together. We hope that it also provides you with an opportunity to deepen your parish connection.

May your family deepen your wonder and joy of living as disciples.

*Margaret*     *Catherine*

Margaret and Catherine

# How can our family journey together?

Sit close to the front at Sunday Mass. Help me with the responses, prayers and songs in the hymn book.

Begin our meals together with the sign of the cross and a thanksgiving prayer. Trace the sign of the cross on my forehead at the beginning or end of each day.

Mark the dates of everyone's baptism on our calendar and celebrate the anniversaries.

Pray with me at bedtime. Pray for all confirmation candidates in our parish.

Invite my sponsor for a meal. Make invitations for people to attend my confirmation celebration.

# 1: Baptized with Water

Dear family,

In our first gathering, we remembered our baptism as we enjoyed God's gift of water. We learned that because of baptism we have new life, and that my baptism and confirmation go together to prepare me to live as part of God's family. Everything that happens in baptism reminds us of what kind of family God's family is and how God means for us to live in the world. Confirmation is God's promise to help me live the new life baptism gives me.

Here are some ways you can help me before our next session.

- Help me find the baptismal font and holy water stoups when we go to church. Remind me to bring my book to church to complete page 7.

- Look for our baptismal certificates and help me complete page 8.

- Help me write my sponsor's name on page 9. Talk with me about this page.

- Say with me the Lord's Prayer on page 10.

Our next session is on ........................................ at ........................................
                          (date)                            (time)

Love,

........................................        ........................................
(My name)                                      (Your name)

Come, Spirit of God

# Water in My Church

Circle the ones that are like the ones in your church.

# Baptism and My Family

Here's a picture of my baptism.

My name: ........................................

When I was baptized: ........................................

My baptism church: ........................................

........................................

........................................
Name

........................................
Date of Baptism

........................................
Church

........................................

........................................
Name

........................................
Date of Baptism

........................................
Church

........................................

8

# Confirmation Moment 1

During my confirmation, my sponsor,

......................................................... ,

will put a hand on my shoulder.

I know I am never alone.

# The Lord's Prayer

Our Father,
who art in heaven,
hallowed be thy name;
thy kingdom come;
thy will be done
on earth as it is in heaven.
Give us this day our daily bread;
and forgive us our trespasses as we
forgive those who trespass against us;
and lead us not into temptation,
but deliver us from evil.

*Amen.*

10

Come, Spirit of God

# 2: Anointed with Oil

Dear family,

In our second gathering, we again remembered our baptism as we enjoyed God's gift of oil. We learned the words *chrism* and *anoint*. At baptism, we are anointed with chrism to show we are now like Jesus.

We learned that God's family has a special job: to continue Jesus' work by bringing God's love to other people, telling people about God's love, praying for them, and showing them God's ways.

God's family has to work together to help each other. The Holy Spirit will also help. Confirmation is God's promise that the Holy Spirit will always be with me to help me.

Here are some ways you can help me before our next session.

- Please help me to find the display of holy oils when we go to church. Remind me to bring my book to church to complete page 12.

- Let's complete together page 13 as you tell me your memories of my baptism.

- Talk with me about page 14 and help me learn my part.

- Let's pray together Psalm 23 on page 15.

Our next session is on ............................................... at ...............................................
     (date)                    (time)

For our next session, please remind me to wear a special piece of clothing.

Love,

...........................................          ...........................................
     (My name)                        (Your name)

# Oils in My Church

Circle the ones that are like the ones in your church.

# Who Celebrated My Baptism with Me?

Priest or Deacon or Parish Leader

Godparent

Godparent

Guests

Help me complete this page.

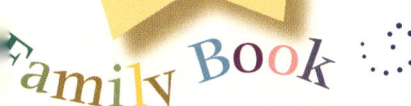

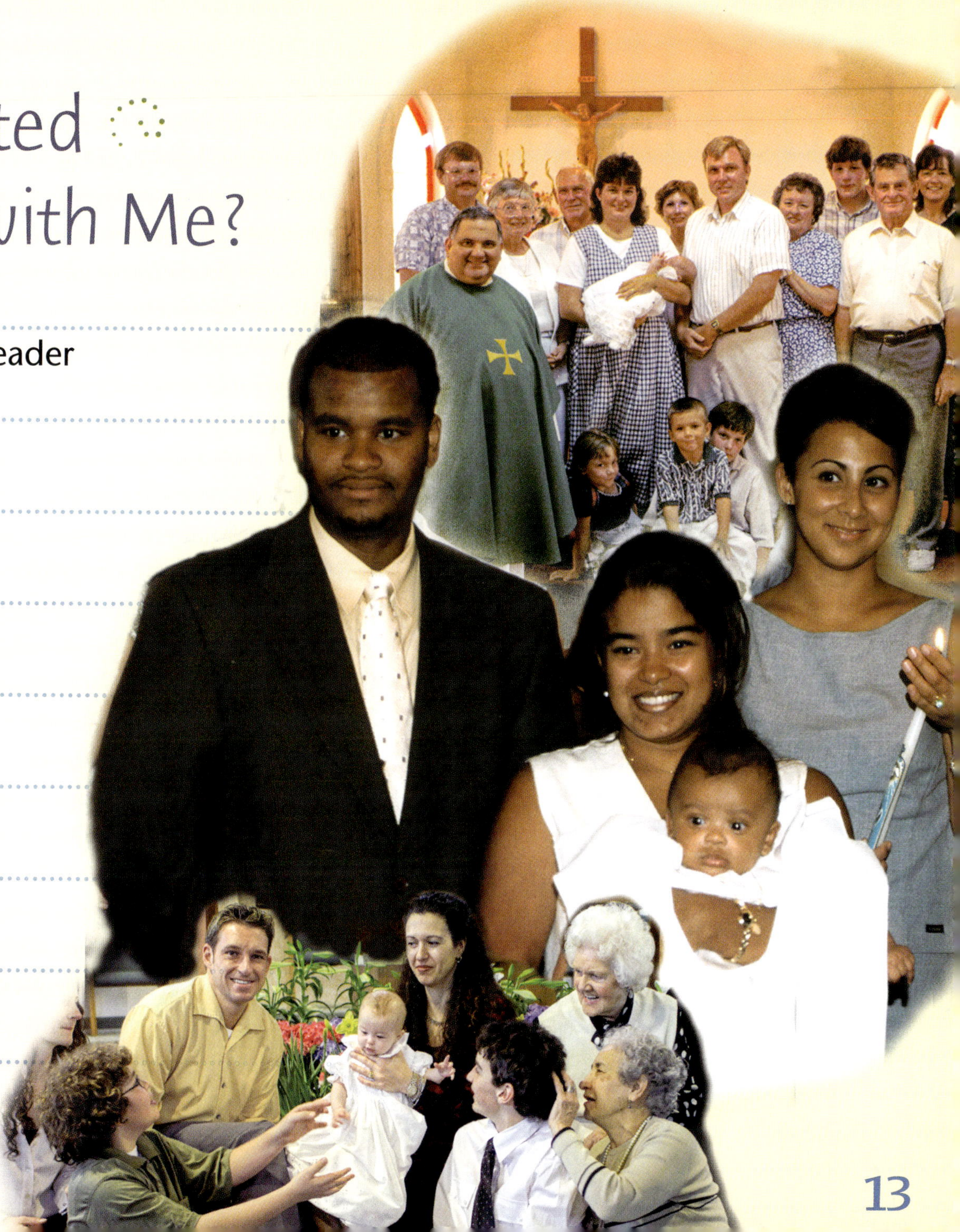

Family Book

# Confirmation Moment 2

During my confirmation I will be anointed.

The bishop will say, " ........................................................... ,

**be sealed with the Gift of the Holy Spirit.**"

I will say,

"Amen."

After I put my name on the line, please help me learn when to say "Amen."

14

Come, Spirit of God

## Psalm 23
(adapted)

Lord, you are my shepherd;
I'll always have everything I need.
You bring me to lie down in green pastures;
you lead me beside calm waters,
and you make me new again.
Lord, you show me the safe path
so that everyone will know your goodness.
Even though I walk through the darkest places,
I don't need to be afraid for you are with me;
your shepherd's staff
makes me feel safe and cared for.
You set a banquet table for me
in the most dangerous times;
you anoint my head with oil;
my cup is full and overflowing.
I'm sure your goodness and mercy shall follow me
all the days of my life,
and I shall live in your house my whole life long.

*Amen.*

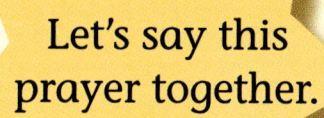

Let's say this
prayer together.

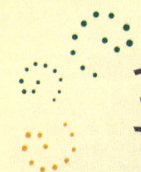

# 3: Clothed in Christ

Dear family,

Did you know that Christ is my invisible clothing that I never take off? I can't wear my baptismal garment forever, but I can take Christ and his cross wherever I go, so his cross is very special for me.

I learned that Jesus' cross was difficult for him, and living as a confirmed Christian can be difficult for me. I also learned that the Holy Spirit gives gifts to help me.

Here are some ways you can help me before our next session.

- Trace the sign of the cross on my forehead at bedtime.

- Talk with me about my pictures on page 17 and tell me your answer to this question:
  "If Jesus were a piece of clothing, what do you think he would be?"

- Join me in finding crosses in my world so I can tell about them on page 18.

- Find my baptismal garment and photos from the day of my baptism and tell me about the photos.

- Talk with me about page 19.

- Let's say together the Prayer of St. Francis on page 20.

Our next session is on ............................................ at ............................................
                                        (date)                                    (time)

Please help me find my baptismal candle so I can bring it to the next session.

Love,

............................................          ............................................
        (My name)                                    (Your name)

16

*Come, Spirit of God*

# Clothed in Christ

If I could be
a piece of clothing,
here's what
I would be.

If Jesus were
a piece of clothing,
here's what
I think
he would be.

# The Cross in My World

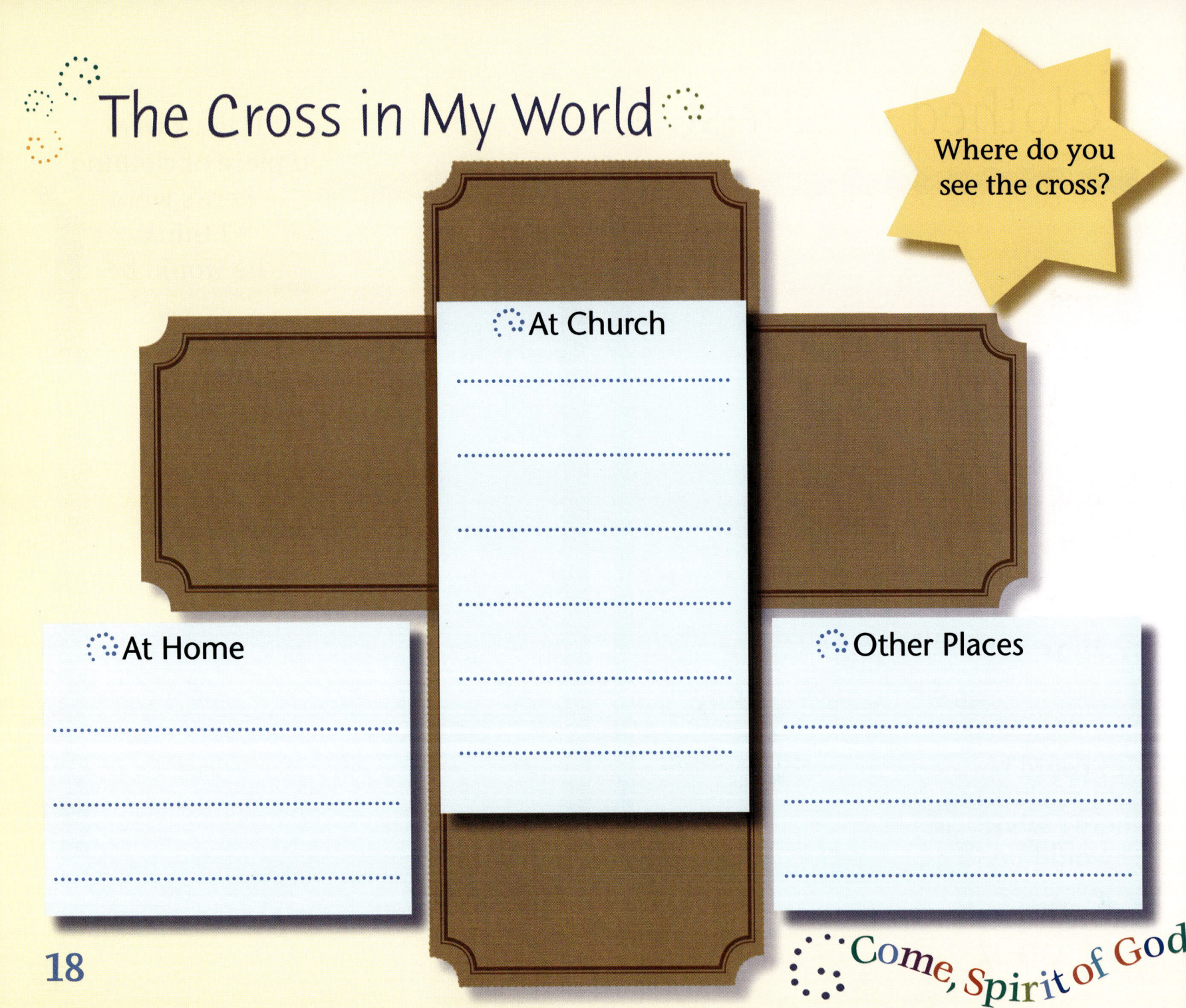

Where do you see the cross?

At Church

At Home

Other Places

Come, Spirit of God

# Confirmation Moment 3

At confirmation, the bishop will say this prayer:

**"Give them the spirit of wisdom**

**and understanding,** *counsel*

**the spirit of right judgement**

**and courage,** *fortitude*

**the spirit of knowledge**

**and reverence.** *Piety*

**Fill them with the spirit**

**of wonder and awe**

**in your presence."**

How will you use these gifts from God?

19

# The Prayer of St. Francis of Assisi

(adapted)

Lord, make me a messenger of your peace.
Where there is hatred, let me bring love;
where there is hurt, let me bring forgiveness;
where there is fear, let me bring faith;
where there is worry, let me bring hope;
where there is darkness, let me bring light;
where there is sadness, let me bring joy.

O Divine Master,
help me not to be selfish.
Help me help others even more often
than I ask for help.
Help me understand others even more
than I ask others to understand me.
Help me love others even more than they love me.

For whenever we give, we receive;
and whenever we forgive, we are forgiven;
and when we die, we are born to eternal life with you.

Let's say
this prayer
together.

Come, Spirit of God

# 4: Enlightened by Christ

Dear family,

Confirmation time is getting close! I am learning how to live in the Christian community and in the world.

I learned I was given a candle at baptism because I have been enlightened by Christ. That means I have the light of Christ in me and the light of Christ can shine from me. The Holy Spirit brings gifts that work with that light. Christ's light and the Holy Spirit's gifts help me know God. These gifts help my faith grow.

Here are some ways you can help me before my next session.

- Let's talk together about being light for one another. Help me with ideas for pages 22 and 23.

- Help me learn my part on page 24.

- Let's say together the prayer on page 25.

- At Sunday Mass, let's go on a candle hunt and find all the candles.

Our next session is on ................................................. at .............................................
                               (date)                                     (time)

Love,

.............................................              .............................................
       (My name)                             (Your name)

# Who Is Light for Me?

Who is a light for you?  Draw a picture to show how.

Write the person's name on the line

and fill in the rest of the box.

..........................................................

is a light for me because

.................................................

.................................................

.................................................

.................................................

.................................................

.................................................

Come, Spirit of God

# I Am Light, Too

Draw candles on the cake to show how long you have been baptized.

On each candle, write the name of someone for whom you can be light.

# Confirmation Moment 4

At confirmation we say again our baptism promises.

**"Do you reject Satan, and all his works,
and all his empty promises?"**

*"I do!"*

**"Do you believe in God, the Father almighty,
creator of heaven and earth?"**

*"I do!"*

**"Do you believe in Jesus Christ, his only Son, our Lord,
who was born of the Virgin Mary,
was crucified, died, and was buried,
rose from the dead,
and is now seated at the right hand of the Father?"**

*"I do!"*

**"Do you believe in the Holy Spirit,
the holy catholic Church, the communion of saints,
the forgiveness of sins, the resurrection of the body,
and the life everlasting?"**

*"I do!"*

Help me learn
when to say
"I do!"

Come, Spirit of God

24

# Glory to God

Glory to God in the highest,
and peace to his people on earth.
Lord God, heavenly King,
almighty God and Father.
We worship you.
We give you thanks.
We praise you for your glory.

Lord Jesus Christ, only Son of the Father.
Lord God, Lamb of God,
you take away the sin of the world:
have mercy on us.
You are seated at the right hand of the Father:
receive our prayer.

For you alone are the Holy One.
You alone are the Lord.
You alone are the Most High,
Jesus Christ,
with the Holy Spirit,
in the glory of God the Father.

*Amen.*

Let's say
this prayer
together.

25

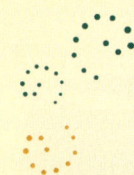

# 5: Awakened to Grace

Dear family,

I learned that at my baptism my ears and mouth were touched, and the family of God prayed that I would be opened to receive God's word and proclaim God's praise. We talked about getting messages from God and about God's dream that we would be a message from God to the world, and a prayer from the world back to God.

Thank you for bringing me to Mass on Sundays. At the Sunday eucharist I use my ears to hear God's word. I use my mouth to say thank you and sing God's praise. I also pray for everyone who needs God's help.

Here are some ways you can help me during the last days of preparation.

- Help me complete page 27.

- Help me learn my part from page 28.

My confirmation will be celebrated on ............................................... at ..............................................

Our last session is on .......................................... at ...........................................

Please remind me to bring my book with me.

Love,

..............................................    ..............................................
      (My name)           (Your name)

# I Can Do It!

Jesus has touched my ears
to receive his word,
and my mouth
to tell it to the world.

**Print a message you have received about God.**

**Print something you would like to say to the world about God.**

# Confirmation Moment 5

After I am anointed
with oil,
the bishop says,
**"Peace be with you."**
I answer,
"And also with you."

Help me
learn when to say,
"And also with you."

28

# Breathe on Me, Breath of God

(adapted from a hymn by Edwin Hatch)

Breathe on me, Breath of God,
fill me with life that is new,
that I may love what you love,
and do what you would do.

Breathe on me, Breath of God,
until my heart is strong,
until I want whatever you want
to do my whole life long.

Breathe on me, Breath of God,
live within my mind,
until every part of me
is wise and brave and kind.

Breathe on me, Breath of God,
and I will live forever with you;
safe within your loving arms,
knowing happiness that's true.

# 6: Confirmed for Life

Dear family,

In our final gathering, we remembered our celebration of the sacraments and learned that God called us to them so we can live fully in the world. At the Sunday eucharist God feeds me with the body and blood of Christ so I can work with Christ and for Christ at home, at school, in our parish, and in our community. I can do this because I have been anointed with the Holy Spirit.

I have thought about what I can do to bring Christ to the world. Look at page 31 with me.

In the coming weeks, remind me to look at this book so I can remember my place in God's family. I can even bring it to church and read it before Mass to help me get ready to celebrate.

Thank you for bringing me into God's family and helping me grow in Christ.

Love,

..............................................
        (My name)

# Bringing Christ to the World

Now is a good time to make some plans for your life as a confirmed Christian. Think about how you and your family will continue to live and grow as members of God's family.

| What we already do | What we will try to do in the future |
| --- | --- |
| ...................................... | ...................................... |
| ...................................... | ...................................... |
| ...................................... | ...................................... |
| ...................................... | ...................................... |
| ...................................... | ...................................... |
| ...................................... | ...................................... |

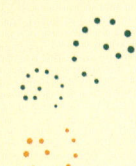

# A Special Letter

Dear wonderful child of God,

Always remember, you are precious in God's sight and God loves you.

*Remember also these words:*

> You were baptized into Christ and have clothed yourselves with Christ.
> Let the same mind be in you that was in him.

> You are part of a royal priesthood, a holy nation, my own people,
> so that you may proclaim God's mighty acts.

> Jesus is the light of the world. Whoever follows him
> will never walk in darkness but will have the light of life.

> You are the light of the world. Let your light shine for others, so that
> they may see your good works and give glory to your Father in heaven.

> Do not worry about what you are to say. The Holy Spirit will guide you
> and remind you of all that I have told you.

Peace be with you.

Come, Spirit of God